Printed in the United States
by Baker & Taylor Publisher Services

The mind is like a computer.
When you put negative thoughts in your mind,
press "Delete."
When you put positive loving thoughts
in your mind, press "Enter."
YOU are in control..."

Gramma Shirah

Title	Author	Publisher
Love	Buscaglia, Leo.	Charles Slack
The Power of Focus	Canfield, Jack.	Prentice-Hall
101 Ways to Enhance Self Concept in the Classroom	Canfield, Jack.	Berkeley
Dare to Win	Canfield, Jack	Berkeley
Chicken Soup for the Soul (The Series)	Canfield, Jack & Hansen, Mark V	Health Communications
Living Your Dreams	Canfield, Jack	Health Communications
Wise Women Don't Worry, Wise Women	Claypool, Jane	Cornucopia
What You Think of Me is None of My Business	Cole-Whittaker, Terry	Harper Collins
The Power of Intention	Dyer, Wayne	Hay House
You Can Heal Your Life	Hay, Louise	Hay House
The Power is Within You	Hay, Louise	Hay House
Feel the Fear and Do it Anyway	Jeffers, Susan.	Penguin
I Can Handle It!	Jeffers, S. & Gradstein, D.	Random House
Redirecting Children's Behavior	Kvols, Kathryn	INCAF
Life Lessons for Women	Marston, Stephanie	Health Comm.
Follow Your Instincts	Monterrey, Lillian.	Monterrey
Understanding Yourself and Others	Reidler, Bill.	Global Relationship
Stand Up for Your Life	Richardson, Cheryl	Free Press
100 Ways to Enhance Self Esteem	Semigran, Candy & Roger, John	MSIA
A Course in Miracles	Schucman	Found. for Inner Peace
I Am Lovable and Capable	Simon, Sid.	Argus
A Return to Love	Williamson, Marianne	Fawcett
Ready, Set, Grow	Wilt, Joy	Free Press
"O" Magazine	Winfrey, Oprah, Ed,	Harpo

"You lend your light to one person, and he or she shines it on another and another and another…"

Oprah Winfrey

"If we want people to know you, you are responsible for communicating yourself to them."

And remember to say,

"I forgive myself for being less than perfect."

... Leo Buscaglia

One of the most wonderful risks I ever took was in writing a letter to Leo Buscaglia. I had seen *"Dr. Love"* (as he was known) on PBS television and read his masterpiece *"Love"* in 1982. He actually answered my letter as if I had known him all my life.

I continued writing him until his death in 1998. I have a wonderful collection of letters from Leo. It is because of him that I'm writing these books. I learned after his death that he answered every letter he ever received in his warm, nurturing and huggable style.

He taught me that we all make a difference to each other. What I have to say might be the very thing that lifts someone else up.

Let people know who you are.

Share your light and love with others. It's up to you.

"Education is the door to freedom, the rainbow that leads to the pot of gold."

"You lend your light to one person, and he or she shines it on another and another and another..."

...Oprah Winfrey.

As everyone knows, Oprah has made significant contributions to our world.
She has always supported the importance of education in helping people grow.

She admires and respects her teachers and she pays them homage.
She also makes it easy for others to pursue their education.

You lend your light... It helps others realize how really significant we all are to each other in ways we might never imagine.

Her message is to reach out to others and give of yourself. Oprah is a tremendous light force on this planet and to me especially.

"Visualize the power of intention…
Recite the seven words that represent the faces of intention: creative, kind, loving, beautiful, expanding, abundant, and receptive."

Wayne Dyer

"Visualize the power of intention.
Recite the seven words that represent the faces of intention:
Creative, Kind, Loving, Beautiful, Expanding, Abundant and Receptive."

"Treat yourself as if you already are what you'd like to become."

...Wayne Dyer

Wayne Dyer's latest book *"The Power of Intention"* is so important. I strongly suggest you read it cover to cover.

The ideas presented stem from his belief we are all spiritual beings in a human form; and that we are all connected to the source of all energy.

My whole journey is without a doubt a tribute to my power of intention.

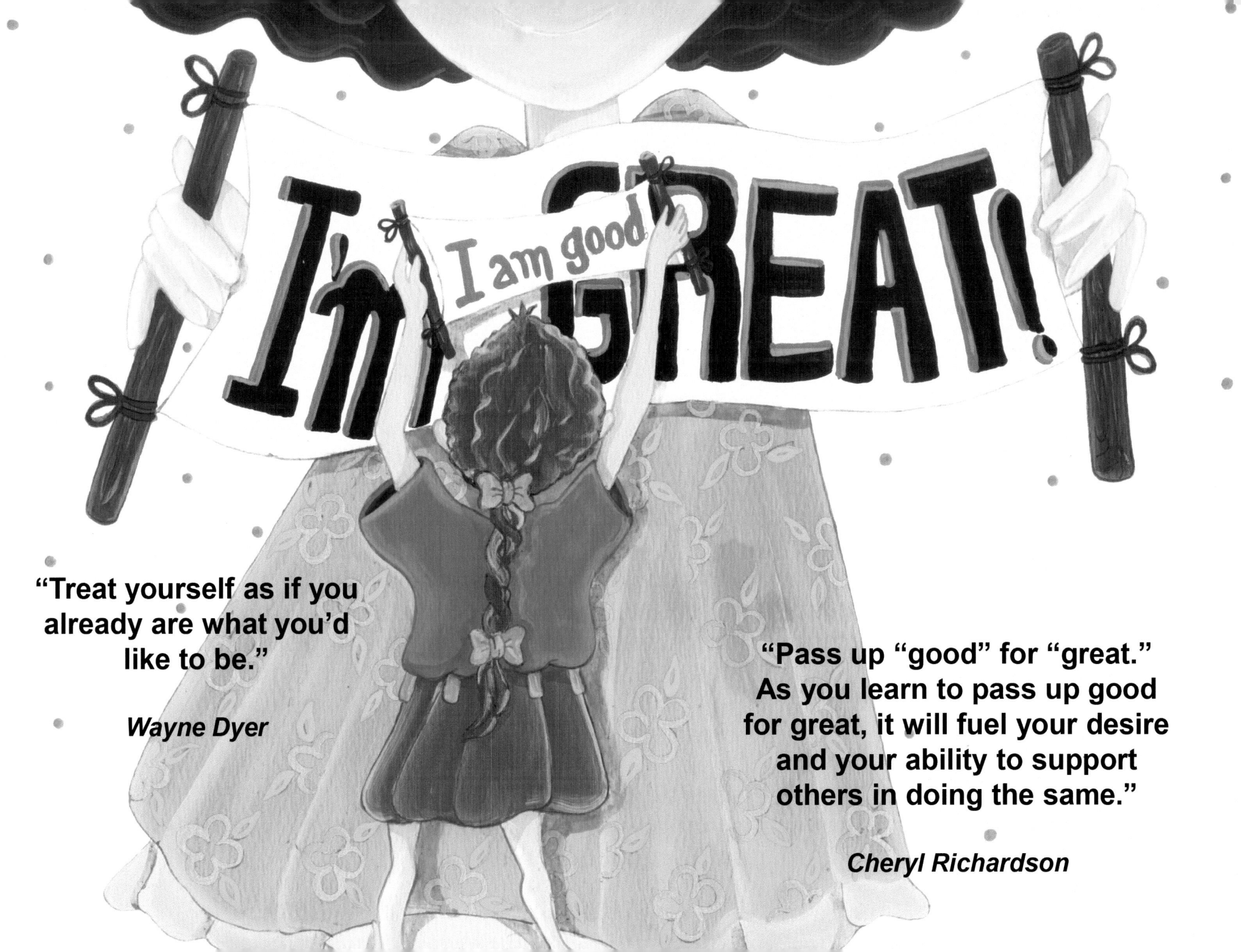

"Treat yourself as if you already are what you'd like to be."

Wayne Dyer

"Pass up "good" for "great." As you learn to pass up good for great, it will fuel your desire and your ability to support others in doing the same."

Cheryl Richardson

"Pass up "good" for "great".
As you learn to pass up good for great it will fuel your desire and your ability to support others in doing the same."

...Cheryl Richardson

This quote by Cheryl Richardson has helped me realize that I often settle for being less than who I could be. Because in the past my sense of worth was low, I didn't recognize and acknowledge my essential goodness, even greatness. I would settle for having, doing and being less in many areas of my life.

I thought of myself as 'just a teacher." I thought this despite knowing in my "head" that being a teacher already has greatness built into it. I had yet to fully put that thought into a feeling in my "heart." Being a teacher means that I am influencing others just being myself. That's awesome when you think about it; and quite a daunting responsibility.

Cheryl Richardson's book *"Stand Up for Your Life"* has a chapter devoted to paying attention to your spiritual standards and values. This requires patience, risk-taking, courage and great faith.

"You are a tremendous force for good in this world.
Every movement you make spreads out like waves from a pebble dropped into a pond.
Encourage yourself, encourage others."

Bill Reidler

"You are a tremendous force for good in this world. Every movement you make spreads out like waves from a pebble dropped into a pond. Encourage yourself. Encourage others."

...Bill Reidler

This is from Bill Reidler's *"Understanding Yourself and Others."* It's the little acts of kindness that cause the ripple effect.

I once taught a class to visualize a peaceful setting. A little girl told me she used the technique to create a calm attitude when she went to the doctor. I hadn't realized that I would influence her to create that effect for herself.

Someone once said to me, "A feeling of unworthiness is only a feeling." So, I was able to change that feeling by creating for myself a more positive feeling. I don't remember who said it but the remark helped me in my life.

Sometimes the very moment we risk making a constructive statement, or reaching out to someone, is the very moment that makes a difference.

"Be your own cheerleader! Encourage yourself!"

Cheryl Richardson

Be your own cheerleader!
Encourage yourself!.

...Cheryl Richardson

Cheryl Richardson's work is all about listening to the voice inside you that sends positive messages. She says to not pay attention to the "chatterbox" voice.

Gramma Shirah learned that even the most accomplished among us do have that chatterbox voice that often blocks us from getting what we want from our life.
Cheryl Richardson gently taught Gramma Shirah to just keep going.

Sometimes we sabotage ourselves from getting what we want by listening to the inner voice of the critic rather than our inner cheerleader.

'"You're never angry for the reason you think..."
from
A Course In Miracles
by Helen Schucman & William Thetford

I have heard and read that statement from so many people. From it I learned to take responsibility for my thoughts and feelings.

This concept is explained very well in Bill Reidler's *"Understanding Yourself and Others"* and in Wayne Dyer's *"Manifesting Your Destiny."* If we get angry because we get an F on a test, we might blame the teacher or the test.

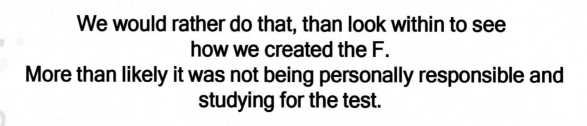

We would rather do that, than look within to see how we created the F.
More than likely it was not being personally responsible and studying for the test.

Sometimes we feel angry because we don't want to admit that we're feeling hurt. Sometimes we feel anger to cover up the powerless feeling. Thoughts create feelings.
We act out our feelings.

"You have a sixth sense inside you.
All you have to do is follow your instincts
to success, wealth, and happiness.
Follow your instincts."

Lillian Monterrey

"In the mind, love is a concept.
In the heart, love is an action."

*John-Roger
&
Candy Semigran*

You have a sixth sense inside you. All you have to do is follow your instincts to success, wealth and happiness.
... Lillian Monterrey

In her book *"Follow Your Instincts,"* Lillian Monterrey encourages her readers to trust their "inner knower" to follow one's heart.
When I first met Lillian Monterrey, I trusted my instincts to get to know her. She also followed her instincts to get to know me. We know we can learn from each other and share what we learn.

As I take my path as Gramma Shirah I have steadfastly followed my instincts. The more work I have done in building my personal sense of self worth and acceptance, the easier it has been for me to make positive choices for my life. I chose to continue to follow my instincts.

No one cares how much you know until they know how much you care.
... Take care of yourself so you can take care of others.
... In the mind love is a concept. In the heart love is an action.

...John-Roger and Candy Semigran

As a teacher and parent, I learned that unless my kids realized that I cared about their well - being, I wouldn't be able to teach very much. By letting others know you care, you can get so much more accomplished. People don't always have to agree about things, they just need to respect each other.
The act of loving goes a long way to unite people.
Sometimes loving is not the easier way.
But in the long run it's the most helpful.

"It is not our arrogance but our humility, which teaches us that who we are is good enough, and what we have to say is valid."

Marianne Williamson

"It is not our arrogance, but our humility, which teaches us that who we are is good enough, and what we have to say is valid."

...Marianne Williamson

I learned from this quote from Marianne Williamson that when we share with people who we really are, we are not being conceited or arrogant. I learned that when I feel good about myself and know my strengths and limitations, that I can honestly give and receive praise and I can give and receive feedback to correct myself along the way. This also tells me that I don't have to be perfect, I am just fine just the way I am.

"It is our light,
not our darkness,
that most frightens us...."

Nelson Mandela
&
Marianne Williamson

Our deepest fear is that we are powerful beyond measure. It is our light, not our darkness, that most frightens us.

...Nelson Mandela & Marianne Williamson

I heard the last quote from Marianne Williamson. She attributed it to Nelson Mandela. This quote holds great significance to me. Much of my shyness, self doubt and fears come from withholding the beauty of who I am and what I have to offer. If this is true of me, it must be true for others because we are basically all the same.

It is this quote that gave me the courage to create Gramma Shirah who speaks for me. Gramma Shirah has lived for 66 years. She experienced much and learned many of life's lessons; and continues to learn. She is ready to share her wisdom and strengths and shortcomings as she shares a lesson learned. Gramma Shirah does this out of love and commitment to herself and others.

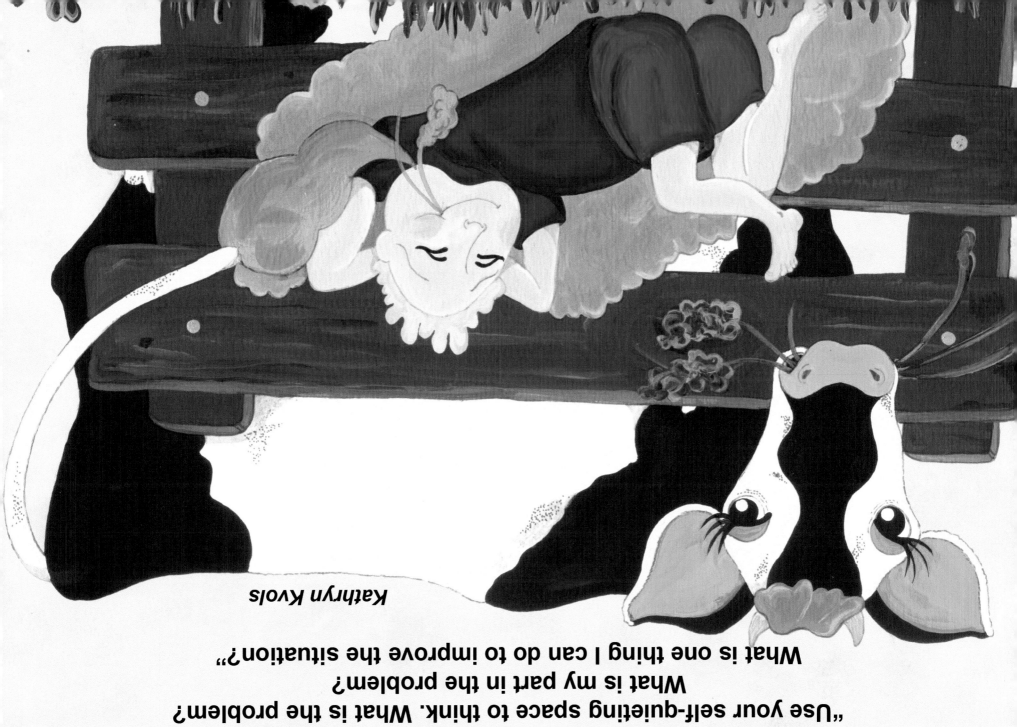

"Use your self-quieting space to think. What is the problem?
What is my part in the problem?
What is one thing I can do to improve the situation?"

Kathryn Kvols

Use your self - quieting space to think. What is the problem? What is my part in the problem? What is the one thing I can do to improve the situation?

...Kathryn Kvols

I learned this incredibly valuable tool from Kathryn Kvols' *"Redirecting Children's Behavior"* and *"Redirecting for a Cooperative Classroom."* I found it very empowering to look at my behavior, which I could change, rather than trying to manipulate and control my children in the classroom.

My life improved, from the application of this tool, outside the classroom as well.

I taught this skill to the children to help them assume responsibility for their part in a conflict.
Their behavior is the only one over which they can truly control.

"I will listen to my fear
to avoid danger."

Joy Wilt

I will listen to my fear to avoid danger.
... Joy Wilt

Joy Wilt reminds us there are times when we could listen to our fear, rather than react thoughtlessly.
To determine a wise action to avoid danger, sometimes it is in our best interest to pay deliberate and considered attention to the fight or flight response.
It is good to *"Feel the Fear and Do It Anyway"* as Susan Jeffers tell us. But, sometimes it is foolish to disregard those signals. We would not recklessly run out in the street when cars are coming.

However, in many instances it is good to take the risk. Ask yourself "What is the worst that could happen?" If it isn't life threatening, tell yourself you can handle it.

Sometimes we create feelings of fear (False Expectations About Reality) to keep us from taking productive action. We are afraid to make a mistake or look foolish. That puts other people in control, rather than under our own self control.

I trust in my ability to handle whatever comes my way.
I'll handle it."
…Susan Jeffers

In her book *"Feel the Fear and Do It Anyway"* Susan Jeffers taught me tools to handle
many of my fears. She taught me that I could re -educate
my mind to face obstacles with confidence. When I tell myself that I can handle whatever
comes my way, I feel less afraid to risk making a mistake.

Her book is often quoted because there are so many powerful and useful tools to enable
one to make decisions, achieve more enjoyment
and make your dreams into a reality.

A children's book that deals with the concept of educating your mind
with positive thoughts is *"The Little Engine That Could."*
When children learn, "I think I can, I think I can, I think I can,"
they have a better chance of reaching their goals.

"You can't change another person;
You can only change yourself."

Louise Hay

You can't change another person, you can only change yourself.
... Louise Hay

This statement by Louise Hay from her *"The Power is Within You"* was transformational to me. It led me into taking responsibility for myself; to stop expecting others to change.

It helps me become less controlling and blaming as a teacher and a mother and a wife. I learned more about how to do this through Kathryn Kvol's *"Redirecting Children's Behavior"* and Bill Reidler's *"Tones That Lead to Love."*

Gramma Shirah would love for you to get this message early. It will help you to take responsibility for being on time, doing your homework and controlling your feelings. You will learn to feel good about yourself. You will improve your self-acceptance.

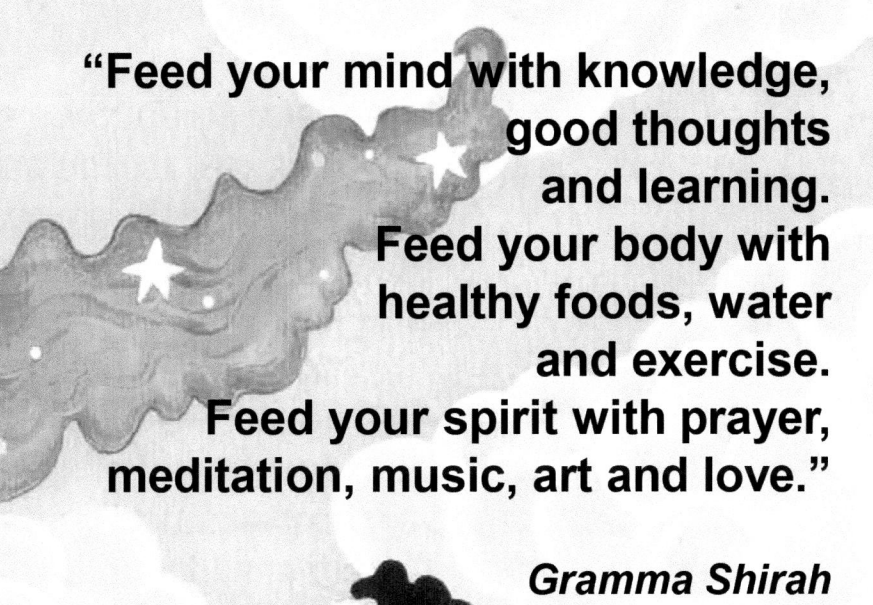

"Feed your mind with knowledge,
good thoughts
and learning.
Feed your body with
healthy foods, water
and exercise.
Feed your spirit with prayer,
meditation, music, art and love."

Gramma Shirah

"If we want a joyous life,
we must think
joyous thoughts.
Use affirmations."

Louise Hay

If we want a joyous life we must think joyous thoughts. Use affirmations.
... Louise Hay

I am very grateful for the works of Louise Hay. In her book *"The Power is Within You"* she explains in detail what an affirmation is and how it works. She says, "Every time you think a thought and every time you speak a word you are saying an affirmation."

I learned how to apply affirmations in my life from Louise Hay's books: *"The Power..."* and *"You Can Heal Your Life."*

Teaching little children how to create and use positive affirmations can be taught by writing affirmations in their "Journals." Children get such a thrill from the creative outlet of writing in their Journals. A journal implies accountability. It is much more than what "big kids" do when they write those "old – fashioned" diaries.

Gramma Shirah experienced Louise Hay's *"I Can Do It"* conference in Atlanta in 2003.
It is very satisfying to see how she exemplifies what she teaches. She is a wonderful role model.

"If you keep on doing what you've always done, you'll keep on getting what you've always got."

Jack Canfield

If you keep doing what you've always done, you'll get what you've always got.
... Jack Canfield

I heard this quote from Jack Canfield. I'm not sure of its original source. He writes about it in *"Chicken Soup for the Soul; Living Your Dreams."*

When I retired from teaching I chose to do some different things, and to do some things differently. I really had to pay attention to what I said to myself.

I realized that although Jack Canfield taught me much, I could only gain my approval and acceptance from myself, not someone else. If I had learned that lesson when I was younger my life would have been less painful.

You will find that much of what Gramma Shirah has to say to you, are sayings she received from others. It is through her voice that you are receiving the messages. What you do with them is up to you.

"No matter what you say or do to me, I am still a worthwhile person."

Jack Canfield

"What you think of me is none of my business."

Terry Cole - Whittaker

No matter what you say or do to me, I am still a worthwhile person
...Jack Canfield

When I first read *"100 Ways to Enhance Self Concept in the Classroom"* I was a First Grade Teacher in Dade County, Florida. One of the authors, Jack Canfield, became my teacher in 1982 while I was working on my own self esteem. The "worthwhile person" saying meant a lot to me because I was learning that my self value came from me and not others' opinion of me. I learned that I was uniquely special and so are you!
If you learn this lesson early, no one can bully you or hurt your feelings. You can learn to get attention and acknowledgement from yourself without depending on others.
You can learn to believe in yourself and accept your shortcomings.
If, however, someone criticizes you, or points out mistakes,
you can learn to accept that as their opinion and choose
to use the criticism or not. You are in charge.

What you think of me is none of my business
... Terry Cole - Whittaker

This statement makes the same point. Don't look outside
yourself for validation.
Your self-esteem is up to you.

"I'm lovable and capable
and so are you…"

Sid Simon

I am lovable and capable. And so are you!
... Sid Simon

Sid Simon's little book for children shows how negative statements erode the self esteem.
It is really important to acknowledge and affirm each other and yourself.
I first met Sid Simon in 1990 at a wonderful conference in Miami called
"A World Safe for Children." He was the keynote speaker and led a workshop.
He is a most loving and accepting man.
He is a teacher's teacher.

Grandma Shirah
says More Words
of Wisdom

by
Shirah Penn
and
Khary Guerra

We are mirrors for each other. What you like about yourself, you like in others.

The End

It's O.K.
to make mistakes,
just learn
from them.

If you appreciate what you have, you will fill yourself with gratitude. Fill your self up with this abundance.

If you are interested in learning you will never be bored. If you are full of wonder, you must be wonderful. And if you are the best you can be, you are mighty terrific.

To reach your goal,
keep going – one step
at a time. Don't just
sit there, do something.
Take responsibility for
your actions.

Picture In your mind what you want to do, to be, or to have. These become your goals. You want to know where you are going, so you can get there.

The secret to being a good
reader is to keep reading.
by putting sounds together
you make works.
By putting words together
you make sentences.
Some words
you just
have to
memorize
**The fat
cat sat
on
the hat.**

If you want to have a friend, you need to be a friend. Friends love and accept each other. Friends are kind and caring. Friends agree and disagree kindly. Friends listen and share feelings.

You need to love yourself
so you can love others.
Take your hands, make a little cup.
Put it over your heart
and fill it up, up, up.
Fill it full of love
and lots of cheer.
Share it with
your family and
friends every
day of the year.

If you want to be as wise as an owl, you need to listen to Mother Goose who says, "The wise old owl lived in an oak. The more he heard, the less he spoke. The less he spoke, The more he heard." "Why can't we all be like that wise old bird?

To order additional copies of this book, contact:
Xlibris
844-714-8691
www.Xlibris.com
Orders@Xlibris.com

ISBN: Softcover 978-1-6641-7224-1
ISBN: EBook 978-1-6641-7223-4

Print information available on the last page

Rev. date: 05/06/2021